DREW BREES
Football Superstar

BY MIKE ARTELL

CAPSTONE PRESS
a capstone imprint

Sports Illustrated KIDS Superstar Athletes is published by Capstone Press,
151 Good Counsel Drive, P.O. Box 669, Mankato, Minnesota 56002.
www.capstonepub.com

 Books published by Capstone Press are manufactured with paper
containing at least 10 percent post-consumer waste.

Library of Congress Cataloging-in-Publication Data
Artell, Mike.
  Drew Brees : football superstar / by Mike Artell.
    p. cm.—(Sports Illustrated Kids, superstar athletes)
  Includes bibliographical references and index.
  Summary: "Presents the athletic biography of Drew Brees, including his career as a high school,
college, and professional football player"—Provided by publisher.
  ISBN 978-1-4296-6565-0 (library binding)
  ISBN 978-1-4296-7305-1 (paperback)
  1. Brees, Drew, 1979– —Juvenile literature. 2. Football players—United States—Biography—
Juvenile literature. 3. Quarterbacks (Football)—United States—Biography—Juvenile literature.
4. New Orleans Saints (Football team)—Juvenile literature. I. Title.
  GV939.B695A77 2012
  796.332092—dc22 [B]   2011001019

Editorial Credits
Christopher L. Harbo, editor; Ted Williams, designer; Eric Gohl, media researcher;
    Eric Manske, production specialist

Photo Credits
Donald Allen, 9 (back)
Sports Illustrated/Bob Rosato, cover (left), 6, 19, 21, 22 (bottom); Damian
    Strohmeyer, 17, 23, 24; John Biever, 2–3, 5; John W. McDonough, cover (right), 1, 14,
    22 (top); Peter Read Miller, 10; Robert Beck, 13; Simon Bruty, 7, 18, 22 (middle)
World Picture Network/Austin American-Statesman, 9 (front)

Design Elements
Shutterstock/chudo-yudo, designerpix, Fassver Anna, Fazakas Mihaly

Direct Quotations
Pages 15, 20, from September 9, 2009, *The Wall Street Journal* article "Drew Brees:
    Stretching Limits" by Jen Murphy, http://magazine.wsj.com

Printed in the United States of America in North Mankato, Minnesota.
032011   006110CGF11

TABLE OF CONTENTS

CHAPTER 1

COOL BREES

In 2010 the New Orleans Saints faced the mighty Indianapolis Colts in the Super Bowl. The Saints struggled in the fourth quarter. But quarterback Drew Brees kept the Colts off balance with quick, short passes. With less than 10 minutes to go, Brees fired a touchdown strike to Jeremy Shockey. The Saints surged to a five-point lead.

Lance Moore scores a two-point conversion.

The Colts could still win with a touchdown. To widen their lead, the Saints tried for two points. Brees took the snap. He zipped a pass to Lance Moore for the score. The Saints now led by seven points.

The clock ticked down as the Colts had the ball. Then the Saints **intercepted** a pass. They scored another touchdown. The Saints were Super Bowl champions!

intercept—to catch a pass by the opposing team

CHAPTER 2

A STAR FROM TEXAS

Drew Christopher Brees grew up in Austin, Texas. In high school he played football, baseball, basketball, and tennis. His best sport was football. In 1996 he led Westlake High School to its first state football championship. He won the Texas 5A Most Valuable Player award that year.

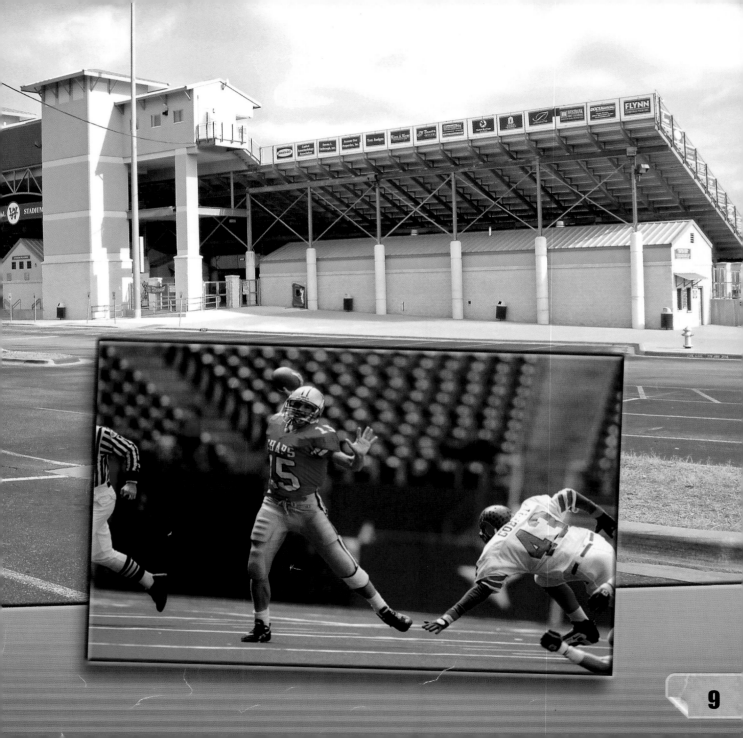

In college Brees became a star at Purdue University in Indiana. In his second season, he started all 13 games. He broke school records for passing **completions**, passing yards, and touchdowns. In his last season, he led the team to the Rose Bowl.

completion—a pass that is successfully caught by a teammate

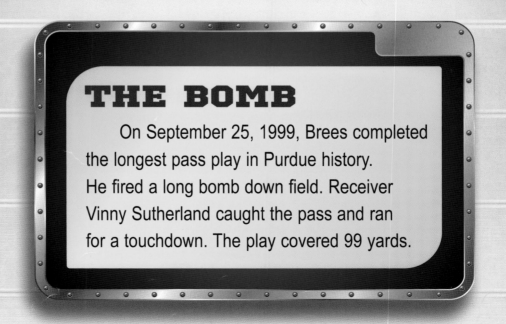

THE BOMB

On September 25, 1999, Brees completed the longest pass play in Purdue history. He fired a long bomb down field. Receiver Vinny Sutherland caught the pass and ran for a touchdown. The play covered 99 yards.

CHAPTER 3

LIFE IN THE NFL

Brees' football skills led him to the National Football League (NFL). In 2001 the San Diego Chargers picked Brees in the second round of the **draft**. As a **rookie** he played one game. In 2002 Brees became the Chargers' starting quarterback. He threw 17 touchdown passes during the season.

draft—the process of choosing a person to join a sports team
rookie—a first-year player

Brees had a shaky 2003 season.
He shared the quarterback job.
The Chargers won only four games.
But Brees bounced back in 2004.
He became the starting quarterback
again. He threw 27 touchdown passes
and only seven interceptions. He was
named **Comeback** Player of the Year.

comeback—to return to a former position or condition of success

"The quarterback position is 90 percent mental and 10 percent physical."—Drew Brees

Brees had another good season in 2005. He passed for 3,576 yards and 24 touchdowns. But a hit in the season's last game hurt his shoulder. The Chargers worried about his throwing arm. After the season, Brees changed teams. He signed with the New Orleans Saints.

BREES DREAM FOUNDATION

Brees started the Brees Dream Foundation to raise money for cancer research and patient care. The group also helps build playgrounds and buy sports equipment for schools.

Brees roared back with the Saints. In 2006 he led all NFL quarterbacks in total passing yards with 4,418. He threw 28 touchdown passes in 2007. In 2008 he threw for 5,069 yards and 34 touchdowns.

In 2009 Brees led the Saints to 13 straight wins. He threw a league-high 34 touchdowns. Brees and the Saints marched through the playoffs. They beat the Colts in the Super Bowl.

CHAPTER 4

DRIVEN TO SUCCEED

Drew Brees is shorter and lighter than most NFL quarterbacks. But few players work harder. In the off-season, he trains three hours a day, five days a week. He gets to practice early, and he stays late. He studies films of other teams. His hard work and strong mind make him a champion.

"The body will only go as far as the mind will take it." –Drew Brees

TIMELINE

1979—Drew Christopher Brees is born January 15 in Dallas, Texas; he later moves to Austin, Texas.

1996—Brees leads the Westlake High Chaps to a perfect 16–0 season and a state football championship.

1998—Brees becomes starting quarterback for Purdue University; he is named Big Ten Player of the Year.

2001—Brees is drafted by the San Diego Chargers as the first pick in the second round.

2006—Brees joins the New Orleans Saints; he leads them to the NFL Championship game.

2008—Brees throws for 5,069 yards; he misses the single-season passing record by only 15 yards.

2010—Brees leads the Saints to a Super Bowl victory; he is named the Super Bowl's Most Valuable Player.

GLOSSARY

comeback (KUHM-bak)—to return to a former position or condition of success

completion (kuhm-PLEE-shuhn)—a pass that is successfully caught by a teammate

draft (DRAFT)—the process of choosing a person to join a sports team

intercept (in-tur-SEPT)—to catch a pass by the opposing team

rookie (RUK-ee)—a first-year player

READ MORE

DiPrimio, Pete. *Drew Brees.* Blue Banner Biographies. Hockessin, Del.: Mitchell Lane Publishers, 2011.

Portman, Michael. *Drew Brees.* Today's Superstars. New York: Gareth Stevens Pub., 2011.

INTERNET SITES

FactHound offers a safe, fun way to find Internet sites related to this book. All of the sites on FactHound have been researched by our staff.

Here's all you do:

Visit *www.facthound.com*

Type in this code: 9781429665650

 **Super-cool stuff!** Check out projects, games and lots more at **www.capstonekids.com**

INDEX